Presented to

_____

By

_____

Date

_____

For Isabella and Emilia,
with love, Daddy
A.L.

Text by Lois Rock
Copyright © 2005 Lion Hudson plc
Illustrations © 2005 Anthony Lewis

North American edition published by Tommy Nelson®, a Division of Thomas Nelson, Inc.

Original edition published in English under the title *A Child's First Story of Jesus* by
Lion Hudson plc, Oxford, England. Copyright © 2005 Lion Hudson plc.

ISBN: 1400305268

Typeset in 20.5/25 Goudy OldStyle BT

Printed in Singapore
05 06 07 08 09 TWP 5 4 3 2 1

A Child's First
Story of Jesus

Lois Rock ✳ Anthony Lewis

Contents

Jesus Is Born

The angel's announcement

The story of Jesus began some 2000 years ago, in a little country on the eastern shore of the Mediterranean Sea. It was a good land, where people could grow barley and flax, grapes and olives. The rolling hills were green when the winter rains fell and bright with flowers in the long, hot summers. Shepherds let their sheep graze there. Jesus' people, the Jews, had made this land their home. However, in the time of Jesus, the Romans ruled their land. It was just a corner of their huge empire.

The Romans had chosen a Jew to be the local king. His name was Herod, and he had a palace in the great city of Jerusalem. He was not a good man, but he had built a beautiful new temple to impress his people. The religious leaders were pleased to have such a lovely building. There in Jerusalem they made sure that God was worshiped according to all the laws and traditions of their people.

To the north of Herod's kingdom was the region of Galilee. Among the hills stood the little town of Nazareth. The huddle of flat-roofed houses made a patch of white against the green and gold of pastures and fields.

In Nazareth lived a young woman named Mary. She was looking forward to her wedding: it was all arranged that she would marry a good man named Joseph.

One day, God sent the angel Gabriel to Mary with a message.

"Peace be with you," said the angel. "God has chosen you to bear a child. You are to call him 'Jesus.'"

Mary was alarmed. Who was this visitor? What did the message mean? It didn't make any sense to her.

"That can't be true," she replied. "I'm not yet married."

"God will make everything come true," said Gabriel, "and your child will be called the Son of God."

Mary shook her head, not yet believing.

"Think about your cousin Elizabeth," said the angel. "Everyone said she was too old to have a child. Yet, by a miracle, she is pregnant."

Yes, that is true, Mary remembered. She thought hard. Then she spoke calmly. "I am ready to serve God in this way," she said.

Soon after the angel's visit, Mary knew for sure that she was pregnant. She went to tell her news to her cousin Elizabeth. The older woman was filled with joy, and at last Mary felt truly happy too.

The Bethlehem baby

In faraway Rome, the emperor Augustus stamped the wax seal on some important letters. Then he ordered that these messages be taken to every part of his empire.

In Nazareth, as in thousands of other towns, everyone began talking about the news.

"We all have to put our names on an official list. The emperor has ordered a census."

"That'll be about taxes, you can be sure. That's the only reason the emperor wants to know about us."

Joseph told Mary the news. Even though she was pregnant and he knew he wasn't the father, Joseph had agreed to marry her. "We'll have to go to my home town to register together," he announced. "That means we will have to go to Bethlehem."

The journey was several days' walking. It was a tiring journey for Mary, for her baby was soon to be born.

She was dismayed when she arrived in Bethlehem. All the rooms for travelers were full. "We will have to make do," explained Joseph. "The only place I can find for us to sleep is a stable."

There, in the place where an ox and a donkey shuffled sleepily, Mary's baby was born.

She wrapped him in swaddling bands and laid him in the manger to sleep.

Out on the hillsides nearby, shepherds were watching over their sheep. Suddenly, an angel appeared to them, shining with all the glory of God.

The shepherds cowered in fear.

"Don't be afraid," said the angel. "I bring you good news. Tonight, in Bethlehem, a boy has been born. He is God's chosen king, the one who will save you and your people from all your troubles. You will find him wrapped in swaddling clothes and lying in a manger."

From out of the darkness, a multitude of angels appeared. "Glory to God in heaven," they said, "and peace on earth."

Then they vanished.

The shepherds looked at one another in bewilderment.

"We must go at once," cried one, "to find out if any of this is true!"

They hurried to Bethlehem. Soon they found Mary and Joseph and the baby in the manger, just as the angel had said. The shepherds told Mary all they had seen.

The wise men and their gifts

In the lands far away to the east, the night sky glittered with stars. Below, some wise men had gathered to study them and to discuss the meaning of what they saw.

"See that star over there," said one.

"I believe it is the sign that a new king has been born—a king so great that we should go and worship him."

The others peered into the heavens. They could see it too.

"Unmistakable!" they agreed. At once, they began to make plans for a journey. Very soon, they set out to follow the star.

It led them first to the great city of Jerusalem, where the Jewish king Herod had a strong and heavily guarded palace.

"Can you tell us where we will find the newborn king?" the travelers asked the townspeople.

Some who heard the questions were Herod's own spies.

When they brought the king the news, he frowned deeply. He spoke in a grim voice. "Bring me those priests who are supposed to advise me," he ordered.

The advisers came at once.

"There is something in the Scriptures that talks about a king God will send," he said darkly. "I want to know more. Where will this king be born?"

"In Bethlehem," they replied. "We can read you the very Scriptures."

Herod narrowed his eyes as he listened. "I understand," he said. "Now I want those star-gazers brought here to see me."

At a secret midnight meeting, Herod asked the men many questions. Then he gave them an order.

"Go to Bethlehem," he said. "That is where our people expect a great king to be born. If you find him, come and tell me where he is; then I can go and . . . worship him as he deserves."

Out in the dark streets, the wise men made their way to the city gates. Then they set out along the road to Bethlehem.

"It's hard to be sure where we're going when it's dark," said one. He sounded a little worried.

"I wonder why Herod was so secretive," added another.

"But LOOK!" said a third. "The star we are following is showing the way!"

The star led the men to a little house in Bethlehem. There they found Mary and the baby.

They gave him three gifts.

The shining gold was a fine gift for a king.

The amber-colored frankincense pieces were something that a priest would burn in ceremonies of worship. Like a priest, this king would bring his people closer to God.

The pale pink myrrh would be used to prepare his body for burial. This king would be remembered not only for his life but also for his death.

The wise men did not go back to Herod. In a dream, an angel warned them that he had evil plans for the child. Instead, they went home a different way.

Joseph also had a warning dream. He heard an angel speaking to him: "Go now, while it is night. King Herod will be looking for the child born to be king. Take Mary and the child to a safe place far away. Go to Egypt and stay there until I tell you it is safe to return."

The little family fled for their lives.

The Boy Jesus

Passover in Jerusalem

Joseph looked happily toward his family. Twelve years had passed since Jesus had been born. The family had made their home in Nazareth. Jesus was a good son—and he was learning to be a good carpenter too.

"And now he is almost grown-up." Joseph sighed as he murmured to himself.

Jesus had finished his years at the little school by the synagogue. The rabbi had taught him his letters, and Jesus had learned how to read from the holy books—the Law and the Prophets. Now he was ready to come on the once-a-year trip to Jerusalem. As usual, Mary and Joseph were going with a crowd of townspeople.

The journey would take several days. At the end they would see the splendid Temple on the hilltop. They believed it was

the best place in all the world for the Jews to
worship God. Then they would enter the city gates,
singing and laughing.

There they would celebrate the festival of
Passover. They would listen again to the old stories
of how God had rescued their people from slavery.
In those days God had made an agreement with
them: they must keep God's laws and God would
always take care of them.

When the festival was over, the people from Nazareth set out for home. They felt like one big family.

"I've been so busy talking, I haven't seen Jesus all day!" exclaimed Mary to Joseph.

"No, neither have I," Joseph replied. "Where is he?"

They began asking their relatives and friends: "Have you seen Jesus? Was he talking to you today?"

Soon they realized that there was a big problem. No one had seen Jesus. Mary looked at Joseph. He was as alarmed as she was.

"We will have to

go back to Jerusalem and find him," they explained to everyone. Their voices wobbled as they struggled not to cry.

After all, Jesus was almost grown-up . . . so maybe he was all right. But maybe he wasn't.

Mary and Joseph hurried back. They went to all the places they had been together. They talked to all the people they had met. For three days they searched.

No one had seen Jesus.

"Let's try the Temple again," said Joseph. "There are so many people in that huge courtyard around it."

25

There, at last, they found Jesus. He was talking with some important rabbis. They were discussing the meaning of the holy books—the Law and the Prophets. He was also giving his own opinions, and the rabbis seemed astonished at his wisdom.

Mary was too upset to be impressed. "Why have you done this to us?" she exclaimed.

Jesus looked surprised. "Why did you have to look for me?" he asked. "Did you not know that I had to be in my Father's house?"

Mary and Joseph shook their heads. His words simply left them bewildered.

Then Jesus went home with them and was a good and obedient son.

Jesus' New Beginning

John the Baptist

Some thirty years had gone by since the time when Jesus was born. Mary could still remember all the amazing things that had happened, starting with the message from the angel.

Now everything seemed to be coming true. Elizabeth's baby, John, had grown up too. He had become a preacher and had chosen to live out in the wilderness. With his long, ragged hair and rough brown cloak he looked liked a prophet of olden days.

Crowds came to listen to what he had to say.

"Get ready for God! Turn away from wrongdoing! Live in the way that is right and good," called John.

"What do you mean?" they answered. "What must we do?"

"Share what you have with those in need," he answered. "Don't cheat and bully to get your own way; instead, be honest and fair."

Some of the people began to talk among themselves. "Do you remember what the holy books say? That one day God will send a king to rescue us—a messiah, a Christ. Do you think this could be him?"

John knew what they were saying. "Listen," he said. "If any one of you decides to turn away from your wrongdoing, I will baptize that person in the water of the River Jordan. But there is someone much greater who will come soon. He will baptize you with God's Holy Spirit."

Jesus in the wilderness

One day, Jesus came and asked John to baptize him. John held him for a moment beneath the water of the River Jordan, then lifted him up into the bright sunshine. God's Holy Spirit came and settled on him in the form of a dove.

A voice spoke from heaven: "You are my own dear Son. I am pleased with you."

After that, Jesus went off into the wilderness alone. For forty days he ate nothing. While he was feeling hungry, the devil came and spoke to him: "If you are God's Son, you could turn the stones into bread."

"No," said Jesus, "the holy books say this: 'People cannot live by bread alone.'"

The devil spoke again: "Picture the kingdoms of the world . . . and imagine being rich and powerful. Worship me, and it can all be yours."

"No," said Jesus, "the holy books say this: 'Worship God alone.'"

Then the devil took Jesus to Jerusalem. "Look," said the devil. "There is the highest point of the Temple. Throw yourself down from it. If you are God's Son, angels will come and save you."

"No," said Jesus, "the holy books say this: 'Do not put God to the test.'"

Then the devil went away.

Jesus in the synagogue

Not long after he had been baptized, Jesus went back to Galilee. One Sabbath day in Nazareth, when everyone had gathered in the synagogue, the leader asked Jesus to take his turn and read from the holy books.

The reading of the day was from the book of the prophet Isaiah.

"The Spirit of the Lord is upon me," he read, "because he has chosen me to bring good news to the poor."

Everyone listened, their eyes fixed on Jesus. He completed the passage, sat down, and said, "Today these words have come true."

"What do you mean?" they exclaimed. "That you are God's chosen one? You're just the son of Joseph!"

They began to hurl insults at him. They jostled him out of the synagogue. Then they grew even angrier. "Let's throw him over a cliff," shouted one of the mob. Somehow, Jesus managed to slip away.

He would never be welcome in his own town again.

33

Jesus in Capernaum

The young fisherman talking to Jesus was quite certain. "You'll be welcome here in Capernaum."

The man's name was Simon. He and his family had a boat down by the harbor. They went fishing each night on Lake Galilee. Today, however, Simon and Jesus were on their way to the synagogue.

Everyone there was eager to hear Jesus speak. Sometimes the rabbis made their religion sound so complicated. When Jesus talked, they felt they really understood more about God and wanted to obey God.

From the back of the hall came shouting. Everyone knew who it was—the man who was gripped by some strange madness. Was the devil in him? people wondered.

"What do you want with us, Jesus of Nazareth?" the man called. "I know who you are—you're God's holy messenger."

Jesus spoke calmly. "Come out of him," he ordered.

At once, whatever had gripped the man left him: he was healed.

As people left the synagogue that day, they could talk of nothing else, and the news spread through the town and beyond.

The news spreads

Jesus went back to Simon's house. Simon's mother-in-law was in bed.

"She has a fever," whispered Simon's wife, "and is very sick. Even if she gets better, she'll need lots of rest."

Jesus went to see the older woman. He spoke to the fever. "Leave her alone," he said.

The woman opened her eyes. She smiled. "I feel better all of a sudden," she said. "Oh—we have a visitor! I must start cooking the meal at once!"

By the time the sun was going down, the news about Jesus' healings had spread. A crowd began to gather outside Simon's house.

"I've brought a friend who has been unwell for years," explained one woman.

"Everyone here has brought someone who is ill," her companion agreed.

With just a touch, Jesus healed all who were in need.

The next day, he got up early and went off to be by himself. People came to find him and begged him to come back to Capernaum.

"Not yet," he replied. "It is now time for me to go and preach in other places too."

Soon he was well known everywhere in Galilee.

Followers and disciples

One day, Jesus came down to the shore of Lake Galilee again. In no time, crowds began to gather.

"Perhaps he will preach to us here, as he does in other places," people were whispering.

They were trying to edge their way closer to Jesus, so that they could be sure of hearing him.

Jesus noticed two boats on the beach. The fishermen had put them there while they washed their nets.

Jesus climbed into a boat and called to one of the fishermen: "Simon—can you push this out for me?"

Simon did so. Jesus stood up in the boat and spoke to the crowds. Everyone could see him and hear him.

When he had finished, he called to Simon, "You and your friends should push the boat into deeper water and let your nets down for a catch."

"It wouldn't be any use!" replied Simon. "We were fishing all last night. We caught nothing."

Jesus kept looking at him.

"Oh, if you like," said Simon, and he called to his friends, James and John.

When they let down their nets, they caught so many fish that they could hardly pull them into the boat.

The fishermen were astonished. How had Jesus known about the fish?

"Don't be afraid at what has happened," said Jesus. "It is a sign to help you understand. From now on, you will be gathering people just as you have been used to gathering fish."

"You will be helping me to bring people closer to God," he explained. "You will be inviting them to be part of God's kingdom."

The men agreed. In this way, four fishermen became Jesus' first disciples. There was Simon (whom Jesus called Peter) and his brother Andrew; James and his brother John.

Not long after, Jesus chose eight more people to be his closest disciples: Philip and Bartholomew, Matthew and Thomas, another James, another Simon (who was a freedom fighter), Judas and Thaddaeus.

There were many others who were friends and followers of Jesus: Mary Magdalene, whom he had healed, was devoted to him. Joanna and Susannah, who were both wealthy women, helped Jesus with gifts of money. Wherever he went, Jesus had many loyal supporters.

Jesus and
His Miracles

The hole in the roof

One day when Jesus was teaching, some of the rabbis and other religious leaders came to listen. They had heard about the new preacher, and they wanted to find out exactly what he was telling people.

That same day, some other men also came to see Jesus. They were carrying a friend who could not move his muscles, and they were using his sleeping mat as a stretcher. The men wanted Jesus to heal their friend.

When they reached the house where Jesus was, they were dismayed. The crowd was so huge that the men could not get near the door. "What now?" asked one. He sounded disappointed and cross.

"I suppose we'll have to see Jesus another time," said another.

"Well, thank you for trying," said the friend on his mat. "Perhaps I wouldn't have been healed anyway."

"I think you would," said a third man. "In fact, I think you will be. Now listen: I've got an idea."

Most houses in the land of Jesus had a flat roof that was used for storing things, and every roof needed steps up to it. Up the men went, carrying their friend.

"Now we must make a hole," said the man.

It was easy to pick away the tiles; it was no problem to scrape away the mud plaster; it didn't take long to break apart the criss-crossed twigs that bridged the gap between the rafters. Then the men let their friend down on his bed right in front of Jesus.

Jesus smiled. He could see that the men believed he could help. He spoke to the man on the bed: "Your sins are forgiven, my friend."

The rabbis and religious leaders gave each other knowing looks. "That's very wrong," they were all thinking. "Only God can forgive sins."

Jesus knew what they were thinking and asked them a question. "What is easier to say—'Your sins are forgiven,' or 'Pick up your bed and walk'? Well, this will show you."

He spoke to the man: "Pick up your bed and walk."

At once, the man who not been able to move did so. "Thanks be to God!" he cried.

Everyone was amazed at what they had seen Jesus do.

The storm on the lake

One evening, Jesus and his disciples went down
to the shore of Lake Galilee.

They climbed aboard one of
the fishing boats.

"Let's go across to the other
side," Jesus said.

The fishermen undid the
moorings and set sail.

Jesus was tired. Within a short while, he had fallen
asleep.

Suddenly, the weather changed. A strong wind
began to blow down from the hills, and the ripples
on the lake became waves. The boat began to pitch
and toss.

"Watch out!" shouted one of the fishermen. "Get
that sail down now."

Half of the disciples struggled with the canvas.
The others began bailing water out of the boat.

"We can't keep up," they shouted. "The waves are

crashing in more water than we can get out."
Someone went and shook Jesus by the shoulder.
"Master! Master! Don't you care? We're about to die!"

Jesus sat up. He looked at his friends, and he looked at the storm. He stood up.

"Be quiet," he said to the waves.

"Be still," he said to the wind.

The storm was gone as quickly as it had come.

Jesus looked at the men. "Where is your faith?" he asked.

They did not know what to say. Slowly they raised the sail and swung it to catch the soft breeze.

They looked at one another with puzzled glances. Who was this Jesus they had agreed to follow? Who could he be, that even the wind and the waves obeyed him?

Jairus and his daughter

"He's coming back now. Look out there, in the middle of the lake. I'm sure it's Jesus' boat."

Down by the shore, the crowds had begun to gather. Jesus, the miracle-worker, had been away, preaching and healing in other places. Many people were eager for him to return. Among them was Jairus, who was one of the leaders at the local synagogue.

Jairus made his way desperately through the crowd. He fell on his knees at Jesus' feet.

"Please come to my house as quickly as you can," he begged. "My only daughter is dying."

Jesus agreed, but it was almost impossible to move. Everyone was pushing and jostling, trying to squeeze their way close to Jesus.

If only I can touch the edge of his cloak, thought one woman, I'm sure I will be healed.

She reached as far as she could, and barely felt the roughness of the woolen cloth before the crowd pushed her back again.

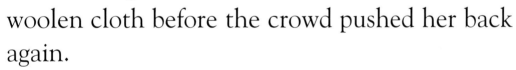

Jesus stopped and looked round. "Who touched me?" he asked.

"Not me," said a young man, pulling his elbows back to his side.

"Nor me," said his friend, as he tried to take a step backward.

Everyone began shaking their heads.

"Master," said Peter, "who can tell who touched you? Look at how many people there are."

"Someone touched me," said Jesus, "and I felt power go out of me."

The woman knew she had been found out. Shaking with fear and embarrassment, she stepped forward and confessed.

Jesus smiled. "Your faith has made you well," he said.

As he turned back to go on his way, a messenger came hurrying up and spoke quietly to Jairus.

"I'm sorry to bring bad news," he said, bending his

head respectfully and solemnly. "Your daughter has just died. You need not bother the teacher any longer."

Jairus began to weep.

"Don't be afraid," said Jesus to Jairus. "Only believe, and she will be well."

When they reached the house, the mourners had already begun to gather. They were weeping noisily.

"There's no need to cry," Jesus told them. "The child is not dead—just sleeping."

"Nonsense!" said one of the women. "We know when someone is dead."

The other mourners began to jeer.

Calmly, Jesus chose Peter, John, and James to come with him. Then the girl's father and mother took him to the room.

Jesus went to the bedside and took the girl by the hand. "Little girl, get up," he said.

At once, she opened her eyes and sat up.

Jairus and his wife clutched one another in amazement, their eyes filling with tears of joy.

"She will need something to eat now," said Jesus.
"Take care of her, but say nothing about what you
have seen."

Food for five thousand

Jesus' disciples had seen their master perform many miracles. One day, he called them all together and said that he was giving them power to work miracles too.

He sent them out into all the villages nearby. They discovered that they were able to preach and heal, just as Jesus did.

When they all met together again, Jesus and his disciples wanted some time with each other away from the crowds. There was no escape! Even though they went to a lonely place, many people followed them.

Jesus saw how eager they were to listen to him. He welcomed them all, telling them about the kingdom of God and what it meant to live as God's own children.

In the evening, the disciples came to speak to Jesus.

"You should send the people away now, so they

can go and find a place to eat and spend the night," they said.

Jesus replied, "You give them something to eat."

The disciples shook their heads. "All we have is five loaves and two fish," they said. "Do you expect us to go and buy food for this crowd? There must be five thousand people here."

"What I want you to do," said Jesus, "is to get the people into groups of about fifty. Then watch me."

When everyone was ready, Jesus took the five loaves and the two fish. He looked to heaven and said a prayer of thanks. Then he broke the food

into pieces and asked the disciples to share it among the people.

Everyone ate as much as they wanted. When the meal was over, the disciples gathered up the scraps. There was enough to fill twelve whole baskets.

A miraculous sight

One day, Jesus stood up from praying and saw his disciples coming to find him. He had a question for them.

"Who do people say I am?" he asked. He knew that everyone was amazed at the things he said and the miracles he had worked.

"Some say you are John the Baptist," they replied. "They know that the king of this region had him beheaded for criticizing the wrong things he did, but still they think you are John come back to life.

"Others say you are a prophet of days gone by, come to live among us again. Perhaps you are Elijah, they say, who stayed faithful to God in spite of many dangers."

"And you?" asked Jesus. "Who do you say I am?"

Peter replied at once. "You are God's Messiah!" he said. "The promised Christ."

About a week later, Jesus went up a mountain to pray. With him he took Peter, John, and James.

The three men fell asleep as they sat waiting. When they woke up, Jesus looked different. His face and his clothes were shining as if they belonged in heaven itself. With him, in the same heavenly light, were two of the greatest prophets of days gone by—Moses, who had given the people laws from God, and Elijah.

As the prophets turned to go, Peter called out, "We could build shelters here, one for each of you."

He wanted the moment to last forever, but even as he was speaking, a cloud came and hid everything in mist. The disciples shrank back in fear. Then they heard a voice: "This is my Son, whom I have chosen. Listen to him!"

Then everything was as it had been—just the three of them and Jesus.

Following Jesus

Like a little child

The disciples all respected Jesus: they knew he had power and authority from God.

But which of them was the greatest? This question led to a big argument. They were jealous of one another, and Jesus knew it.

He beckoned to a child to come and sit next to him. Then he spoke to his disciples: "Whoever welcomes this child in my name welcomes me; and whoever welcomes me also welcomes the one who sent me. For the one who is least among you all is the greatest."

Time and time again, Jesus tried to make his disciples understand: none of his followers should think of themselves as more important than anyone else.

"The greatest among you must be like the youngest," he said, "and the leader must be like the servant. I have set the example. In the things I do, I act like a servant to all of you."

Counting the cost

"If you want to follow me," explained Jesus, "you must love me more than anything else—even more than your family and your own life.

"Imagine you are planning to build something—a tower, perhaps. The first thing you must do is to sit down and work out what it will cost. You need to know if you have enough money to finish the job. If you don't, you may get as far as laying the foundations, but then you will have to stop.

"People will come and laugh. 'Look,' they will say, 'this person began to build a tower but can't finish it.'"

He went on to explain that people should think hard about the cost of following him before they started

making him promises. He needed his followers to
be ready to give up everything for the sake of God's
kingdom.

Hard work

Jesus explained that his followers would have to work hard. After all, they were choosing to be God's own servants.

"Imagine that you hire a servant to help on the farm. In the day, you send him out to plow the fields or to look after the sheep.

"When he comes in from the fields, do you tell him to hurry and eat his meal?

"Of course not! He is still at work. 'Go and prepare my supper, then put on an apron and serve at the table while I eat,' you say. 'After that, you can have your meal.'

"You, too, must be ready to serve God at all times. When you have done all you have been told to do, you should say, 'We are ordinary servants; we have only done our duty.'"

Ready to listen

One day, Jesus and his disciples came to a village. Two sisters who were both friends of Jesus lived there. Their names were Mary and Martha.

Martha welcomed Jesus into her home. Then she went back to all the many jobs that had to be done: sweeping and cleaning, fetching water and preparing food. There was no time to waste in a busy day.

Mary sat down in the room where Jesus was teaching. She wanted to listen to all he had to say.

Martha suddenly felt very cross. She went over to Jesus.

"Don't you care that my sister has left me to do all the work? Tell

her to come and help me!"

Jesus answered her, "Poor Martha! You worry about so many things, but just one is important. Mary has made the right choice."

Listening to Jesus was more important than all the work that kept Martha so busy.

Another time, Jesus said this: "Listen, everyone. If you are tired from all the stress and worry of life, come and follow me. I will show you a different way to live your lives. You will find it is easy. I promise you it will never be too difficult for you to follow me."

Jesus the Teacher

True happiness

Jesus wanted people to understand how much God loved them. He said that God's love included everyone—even those who thought they were nobodies.

"Happy are those of you who are poor," he told them. "The kingdom of God is yours.

"Happy are those of you who are hungry. You will

be given everything you need to satisfy all your longings.

"Happy are those of you who are sad now. God will change everything, and you will laugh for joy.

"Happy are those of you who get into trouble for being my followers. In heaven, you will have a great reward.

"Beware if you are rich and popular and have everything you need for a comfortable life. You have had your blessings already. You will be left with nothing."

Love your enemies

Jesus also told people that they were to love one another just as much as God loved them.

"You must love your enemies," Jesus told his listeners. "Do good things to those who hate you, and pray for the people who try to hurt you.

"If someone asks for something, give it to them. If someone takes what is yours, do not demand to have it back.

"Do for others just what you want them to do for you.

"Even the worst wrongdoers are kind to the people who are kind to them. You must do more than that.

"Love your enemies and do good to them; lend and expect nothing back. God will reward you.
"You must be as kind and as forgiving as God is."

Hearing and doing

"It is not enough just to listen to what I say," explained Jesus. "You must also obey what I tell you.

"Imagine a man who carefully builds his house. He puts the foundations on solid rock. Even when it rains so much that the river floods, his house is safe. Nothing can shake it.

"If you obey my teaching, then you are like that man. But if you hear my teaching and do not obey it, then you are like a man who builds carelessly. He does not bother to build strong foundations. When it rains so much that the river floods, his house is washed away . . . and what a crash it makes!"

The story of the good Samaritan

One day, a teacher of the Law came to see Jesus.

"Teacher," he asked, "what must I do to gain eternal life?"

Jesus knew the man was trying to trap him into saying something that made him look like a bad teacher. "You tell me what our holy books say," he replied.

"They say, 'You must love God with all your heart, with all your soul, with all your strength, and with all your mind,' and also, 'You must love your neighbor as you love yourself.'"

"You are right," said Jesus.

But the teacher of the Law wanted to ask something more. "Who is my neighbor?" he said.

So Jesus told a story.

"There was once a man who was going from

Jerusalem to Jericho. Suddenly, fierce bandits who lived in the hills ambushed him. They beat him up, took all he had, and left him for dead."

"It so happened that a priest from the Temple was going that way. He saw the man, but he walked by on the far side of the road.

"Next came a Levite, a helper at the Temple. He saw the man lying in the road and walked over to take a closer look. Then he too hurried on.

"Soon a Samaritan came along."

The teacher of the Law gave a slight scowl. A priest and a Levite were both very respectable religious people. The people from Samaria were not.

Jesus went on with his story.

"The Samaritan saw the man and felt very sorry for him. He went over to him, cleaned his wounds, and put bandages on them. Then he lifted the man onto his donkey and took him to an inn. There he gave him all the care he needed."

"The following day he paid the innkeeper two silver coins. 'Please take care of this man for me,' he said. 'If it costs more, I will pay the extra when I am here next.'"

Jesus turned to the teacher of the Law. "In your opinion, which of the three acted like a neighbor to the man who was attacked?"

The man's scowl had deepened. Jesus had not said anything he could criticize.

"The one who was kind to him," he admitted, rather sulkily.

"Then you go and do the same," said Jesus.

Jesus' prayer

Jesus often got up early to spend time praying alone.

"Please teach us to pray," one of the disciples asked him.

Jesus replied, "When you pray, go to a quiet place where you can be alone. Don't use lots of words. God already knows what you need. Simply say this:

'Father:
May your holy name be honored;
may your kingdom come.
Give us day by day the food we need.
Forgive us our sins,
for we forgive everyone who does us wrong.
And do not let us be tempted to do bad things.'

"Remember," said Jesus, "to keep on praying.

"Imagine that a friend comes to visit late one evening and you have run out of food. You hurry to your neighbor's and bang on the door.

"The only answer is an angry shout. 'Go away! I've locked up for the night. My family and I are all in bed now.'

"Even so, you can be quite sure that if you keep hammering on the door, your neighbor will get up to answer you.

"So remember this when you pray: ask, and you will receive; seek, and you will find; knock, and the door will be opened for you.

"Those of you who are parents know that you always try to give your children the food they want. If you, with all your faults, are good to your children, just think how much your Father in heaven wants to give you good things—even the gift of the Holy Spirit."

The story of the lost sheep

All kinds of people liked to listen to Jesus. Some were very respectable; others were not. Among the outcasts were tax collectors. They collected money for the Romans and cheated their own people. The religious leaders did not approve of mixing with them.

"If Jesus were a trustworthy teacher, he would not speak to them. As it is, he even eats with them— and that makes him as unworthy as they are."

Jesus told them a story.

"Imagine that one of you has a hundred sheep. One day, you notice that a sheep has gone missing. There are only ninety-nine left.

"What do you do? You leave the ninety-nine safely in the pasture, and you go looking for the one that is lost."

"At last you find it, and how glad you are. All the long hours of searching seem worthwhile. You don't notice how tired you are. You don't mind that your feet are aching. You could dance for joy.

"So you pick up the sheep and lay it on your shoulders. Gently you carry it home to the flock. Once it is safely back in the sheepfold and the gate is shut, you call to all your friends and neighbors, 'I found the sheep that I lost! I am so glad that I want to celebrate. Come to my home—I'm having a party!'

"It's a bit like that with God," explained Jesus. "There is more joy in heaven when one person who has lost his way in life turns back to God than over ninety-nine respectable people."

The story of the loving father

Jesus told this story to help people understand more about God's love.

There was once a man who had two sons. He also had a prosperous farm, and his two sons could look forward to a comfortable future.

However, the younger one was impatient to enjoy all the good things of life. "I don't want to wait till you're dead to have my share of your property," he told his father. "I want it now."

The father agreed to give it to him. As soon as he could, the son sold his share for money. He went to live in a city far away.

"I can afford all the luxuries I want," he said to himself. He enjoyed spending lavishly.

Meanwhile, farmers everywhere were having a bad time. The harvests failed. The price of food soared; the price of everything soared. In a very short time, the young man had used up all his money. He had nothing left to live on.

Paid work was hard to find. He ended up looking after pigs. He was so hungry that he wished he could eat the bean pods he had to feed the animals.

As he sat there, he came to his senses. "My father's workers live better than this," he said to himself. "I will go back to my father and say this: 'I have done wrong and I am sorry. I don't deserve to be treated as your son, but please hire me as a worker.'"

He set out at once. While he was still a long way from home, his father saw him coming. "My dear son!" he cried. He ran to greet him, threw his arms around him, and kissed him.

The son hung his head. He made his apology, but his father didn't seem to be listening.

"Hurry!" he called to his servants. "Fetch him good clothes and shoes and dress him as a son of mine deserves. And go and slaughter our prize calf: I want a feast to celebrate his return."

The elder son was out working in the fields. As he trudged home, he heard music and dancing.

"What's going on?" he asked a servant.

When he heard that it was a party for his wayward brother, he grew angry. He went to his father in a temper. "I was loyal to you all this time!" he shouted. "You never did anything like this for me!"

"My son," the father answered, "everything I have is yours. But we must celebrate and be happy because your brother was dead, but now he is alive; he was lost, but now he has been found."

The Road
to the Cross

On the way to Jerusalem

One day, Jesus spoke privately to his twelve disciples. "It is time for us to go to Jerusalem for Passover. Everything the prophets foretold will come true there."

He talked about dying and rising again, but the disciples did not understand.

The way to Jerusalem went through Jericho. As Jesus came near to the city, a blind beggar by the side of the road heard the crowds.

"What is going on?" he asked.

"Jesus of Nazareth is coming!" they answered.

The blind man began to shout, "Jesus, son of David! Take pity on me."

People told him to be quiet, but the more they scolded, the more he shouted.

Jesus stopped and asked for the man to be led to him. "What do you want?" he asked.

"I want to see again," the man replied.

"Then see!" replied Jesus. "Your faith has made you well."

At once the man could see.

Zaccheus

The chief tax collector in Jericho was named Zaccheus. Like many tax collectors, he charged people much more than he had to. In this way he had made himself very wealthy—and much disliked.

Zaccheus was very short. He wanted to see Jesus but could not because of the crowds in front of him. Determined, he ran ahead and climbed a tree.

When Jesus passed that way, he looked up.

"Hurry down, Zaccheus," he said. "I need to stay in your house today."

Zaccheus was overjoyed. He clambered down and gave Jesus a splendid welcome.

Outside, the crowds started grumbling. "Jesus shouldn't be visiting a person like Zaccheus," they complained.

But after Zaccheus had spent time with Jesus, he was a changed man. He made an announcement: "Listen! I am going to give half my belongings to the poor, and if I have cheated anyone, I will pay

them back four times what I overcharged."

"Today, you have been saved," replied Jesus.
"I came to look for people who were lost and
to rescue them from all their wrongdoing."

Entering Jerusalem

Jesus journeyed on. When he came to the Mount of Olives, just outside the city of Jerusalem, he gave two of his disciples instructions about where to find a donkey.

They brought it to Jesus and threw their cloaks on its back. Then Jesus rode toward Jerusalem. People threw their cloaks into the road to make a soft path for the donkey to walk on.

At the place where the road went down into a valley, the crowd began to shout, "God bless the king!"

Jesus went to the Temple. In the courtyard, merchants were selling animals to sacrifice at the Passover festival. Others were changing money into the special coins needed to pay the Temple offering. There was a lot of shouting and haggling.

Jesus saw what they were doing, and he was angry. "The holy books say that God's Temple is to be a house of prayer," he told them. "You have turned it into a den of thieves."

Suddenly, he began to push the tables over. Scattered coins ran along the paving stones and some of the animals began to run away. "Get out!" Jesus cried to the merchants.

The religious leaders were furious.

"How dare he?" they fumed. "Is he trying to make people think he is God's chosen king?

"The people he spends time with would believe any nonsense—they are just wrongdoers who disobey our holy laws. That man's teaching is a disgrace!

"We must get rid of him," they agreed. "But we will have to arrest him secretly, when the crowds who adore him so much aren't around."

They were astonished when someone came and gave them the chance they wanted: one of Jesus' disciples, Judas Iscariot. In return for money, he told them where they could arrest Jesus quietly.

The last supper

The special day for the Passover meal arrived. Jesus gave Peter and John instructions about the upstairs room where they were to get everything ready.

At the meal, Jesus took a cup of wine. He gave thanks to God and said, "Take this and share it among yourselves. I tell you that from now on I will not drink this wine until the kingdom of God comes."

Then he took a piece of bread. He gave thanks to God, broke it, and gave it to them, saying, "This is my body, which is given for you. Do this in memory of me."

He also gave them the cup of wine after the supper. "This cup is God's new covenant," he said. "It is a promise sealed with my blood, which is poured out for you."

Not long after, Judas Iscariot slipped away. The others began an argument about which one of them was the most important.

Once again, Jesus had to remind them that they should not be acting in this way.

"All of you will have your loyalty to me tested soon," he warned them. "I have prayed for you, Simon Peter, that your faith will not fail."

"It won't," boasted Peter. "Not ever. I'll go to prison with you. I will even die with you."

"Before this night is over," said Jesus, "you will say three times that you do not know me."

Jesus and the eleven disciples went out of the city and across a narrow valley to the foot of the Mount of Olives. The quiet olive grove called Gethsemane was a safe place for them to avoid being noticed.

All alone, through the dark and shadowy night,

Jesus prayed to God. "Father," he pleaded, "take this suffering from me."

He waited and listened. The night breeze blew through the leaves. He knew in his heart what God was telling him. "I will do what you want," he agreed.

Jesus went back to where the disciples were. They had fallen asleep.

Suddenly, Judas arrived, leading a crowd of armed men and religious leaders. He greeted Jesus with a kiss. At once, the soldiers grabbed Jesus. There was a scuffle, and swords were drawn . . . but Jesus did not want a fight. It was not his way to be violent. Instead, he let himself be led away.

Peter

Outside the high priest's house, Peter sat in the courtyard. He was warming himself at the fire there. He had no idea what was happening to Jesus. Somewhere inside, he imagined, the religious leaders were questioning Jesus. He knew they wanted to prove him guilty of some crime so that they could ruin his reputation and then silence him forever.

One of the servant women saw Peter. "This man was with Jesus," she announced to her fellow servants.

Peter was startled. "I don't even know him," he protested. The servants eyed him curiously.

A while later, a man noticed him. "You there—you were one of that band of Jesus' people, weren't you?"

"No, I wasn't," said Peter curtly. The man raised his eyebrows. He didn't look convinced.

An hour later, another man came up. "There's no doubt this is one of Jesus, friends," he said. "Anyone

can tell he's from Galilee. Just listen to his accent."

"I don't know what you're talking about!" Peter's voice was angry. He punched one fist into the other to make his point.

At that moment a cock crowed. The night was over.

Peter remembered what Jesus had told him. He went outside and wept.

Condemned

The following day, the priests met together to talk about Jesus.

"We can all agree on one thing," they said. "He is causing trouble for our people and our religion. It will be best to get rid of him."

They needed the approval of the Roman governor, Pontius Pilate. Only he was allowed to condemn an accused person to death.

They took Jesus to him. He didn't understand the local religion or what the Jewish priests were so upset about. However, he agreed to question Jesus: after all, it was his job as governor to root out troublemakers.

Even when he questioned Jesus, he could not find any wrongdoing that deserved the death penalty.

He gave the priests his verdict. "I shall have the

man whipped and let him go," he said.

By now a crowd had gathered: a noisy, angry crowd who had come to demand that Pilate keep the Passover tradition and let one prisoner go free.

Pilate offered to release Jesus. "Crucify him, crucify him!" they shouted. "Set Barabbas free instead! He's the one we want!"

Barabbas was in prison for murder. Pilate hesitated, but the crowd grew louder. He couldn't risk an uprising.

"As you wish," he said. "Do what you like with Jesus."

When Judas heard the news, he realized what a terrible thing he had done.

Crucified

The Roman soldiers were given their orders at once. As the morning sun rose, Jesus and two other prisoners were led to the place of execution. Each carried the wooden beam on which they must die. There, on a hill outside the city, they nailed Jesus to his cross. Above him, a notice declared his crime:

"This is the King of the Jews."

Even as Jesus hung there dying, he looked at the people who were responsible for his crucifixion.

"Forgive them, Father," he said. "They don't know what they are doing."

At about twelve o'clock, the sun stopped shining, and for the next three hours the sky was eerily dark. Then Jesus cried out, "Father, in your hands I place my spirit," and he died.

A wealthy man named Joseph, who came from Arimathea, hurried to see Pontius Pilate. He was a member of the council that had condemned Jesus, but he had not agreed with what they had decided. However, because he was an important man, Pilate listened to his request: "Let me take the body of Jesus. I will arrange for it to be buried."

Pilate gave his permission, and Joseph had Jesus' body taken from the cross, wrapped in a linen sheet, and laid in a new tomb cut into solid rock.

Some of the women who had followed Jesus came to watch. "It's too late to bury the body properly," they whispered. "It's Friday, and the Sabbath day of rest begins at sunset. We can come back on Sunday morning."

Joseph ordered the round stone door to be rolled over the entrance to the tomb. Night was falling.

The Resurrection

Sunday morning

Very early on Sunday morning the women went back to the tomb. They carried with them the spices they needed to prepare Jesus' body for a proper burial.

"The stone door will be hard to move," whispered one. "I hope we'll be able to manage it."

When they arrived, they found that the tomb was open!

"What has happened?" they gasped in dismay.

Trembling, they stepped inside. The body had been laid on a stone ledge. It was gone.

"Who has done this—and why? Do you think they might still be near?" They looked around fearfully.

Suddenly, two people in bright shining clothes appeared next to them.

"Why are you looking among the dead for one who is alive?" they asked. "He is not here. God has raised him to life."

Then the women remembered. Jesus had spoken of things like this. Maybe the unbelievable really was coming true.

They hurried to tell the disciples. Peter ran to see for himself. What was making the women tell such a story?

He found the tomb empty! What was going on?

That same day two followers of Jesus left Jerusalem. They were walking home to Emmaus, feeling tired and forlorn.

They could think of nothing but Jesus—his sad death and the wild rumors about his tomb.

Along the way, a man joined them and asked what they were talking about.

"You must be the only person in Jerusalem who doesn't know!" they exclaimed, and they told him all the news.

"All of that is what the prophets of our people foretold," replied the man calmly. As they walked along, he explained what he meant.

His words were convincing: he made it sound as if all the sad and puzzling things that had happened were part of God's own plan.

As they reached Emmaus, the evening sky was darkening.

"Stay with us," said the two travelers.

At the meal, the stranger took the bread, said the blessing, and shared the food.

Then they understood. "Jesus!" they exclaimed. But, all of a sudden, he was gone.

The two travelers raced back to Jerusalem to tell the other disciples. "We have seen the Lord!" they said. "The rumors were true! Listen! You have to believe us!"

As they were telling their news, Jesus appeared among them. "Peace be with you," he said.

Then he showed them his wounded hands and feet. "Give me something to eat," he said. "I will show you I am not a ghost."

As they sat together, Jesus explained, "Remember, I told you that all these things would happen to the Messiah: that he would suffer and die and rise three days later.

"Now all that is done. Now it is time for you to continue the work I have begun. I want you to go on spreading the message about God's forgiveness to everyone in the world—and to begin right here in Jerusalem. Wait a while, and God's Holy Spirit will give you all the courage and wisdom you need."

125

Jesus led his disciples out of the city. On a hill nearby, he raised his hands and said a blessing.

Jesus was taken up into heaven. His disciples saw him no more.

Jesus had done all that God's Son had to do. His followers had the job of spreading the good news about God's kingdom: how everyone could become God's own child and take their place in heaven.